Education in the USSR

By Delbert Long and Roberta Long

Library of Congress Catalog Card Number: 80-82681
ISBN 0-87367-148-1
Copyright © 1980 by the Phi Delta Kappa Educational Foundation
Bloomington, Indiana

This fastback is sponsored by the Columbia University Chapter of Phi Delta Kappa, which made a generous financial contribution toward publication costs. In sponsoring the fastback, the chapter wishes to honor Miss Bessie Gabbard, a member of the Board of Governors of the Phi Delta Kappa Educational Foundation.

TABLE OF CONTENTS

The Goals of Education

Sixty-two years ago, in "10 days that shook the world," Vladimir Ilyich Lenin and his followers overturned the provisional government of Russia and established the world's first Communist government. Few people thought the government would survive. The war with Germany had brought the country to its knees economically and politically, and the subsequent civil war intensified the famine, misery, and political chaos that reigned throughout the land. Yet—as if to vindicate Peter the Great's conviction that Russia is "a country in which things that just don't happen happen"—Lenin and his small band of revolutionaries did survive. Lenin, and later Stalin, Khrushchev, and Brezhnev, turned with a vengeance to carrying out the work started by Peter the Great: to transform a backward country into a great power. It was no small task, as Stalin pointed out in 1934. In justifying the necessity of quickly industrializing the country at all costs, Stalin said:

> To slacken the tempo would mean falling behind. And those who fall behind get beaten. But we do not want to be beaten. No, we refuse to be beaten. One feature of the history of old Russia was the continual beatings she suffered because of her backwardness. She was beaten by the Mongol khans. She was beaten by the Turkish beys. She was beaten by the Swedish feudal lords. She was beaten by the Polish and Lithuanian gentry. She was beaten by the British and French capitalists. She was beaten by the Japanese barons. All beat her because of her backwardness, military backwardness, cultural backwardness, political backwardness, industrial backwardness, agricultural backwardness. They beat her because to do so was profitable and could be done with impunity.[1]

To overcome this backwardness Soviet leaders from Lenin to Brezhnev have relied heavily on their system of education. In their

6

judgment education is a vital instrument of state policy. As Lenin put it, "The school must become a weapon of the dictatorship of the proletariat." Stalin was even more explicit. "Education," he said, "is a weapon whose effect depends on who holds it in his hands and who is struck with it."[2] In the USSR, education, as well as all other aspects of Soviet life, is in the hands of the Communist Party, or more accurately in the hands of Brezhnev, Kosygin, and nine other members of the executive committee of the Party, the Politburo. Present members of the Politburo would no doubt agree with Nikita Khrushchev's description of the role of the Party. "The Communist Party," he said, "is the guiding force of socialist society. It expresses the will of the entire Soviet people . . . and the Party will remove from the path of Communist construction everything that stands in the way of the people's interests."[3] The interests of the people are best served by Party members because only they, presumably, understand the truths of Marxism-Leninism and how these truths can be utilized in building a society based on the Communist principle: "From each according to his ability; to each according to his needs."

Marxism-Leninism, it should be noted, is not a philosophy but an ideology. The aim of philosophy is understanding. The aim of ideology is action. As Karl Marx put it, "Philosophers have merely interpreted the world in various ways; the really important thing is to change it." Accepting this dictum, Party leaders use Marxism-Leninism as a convenient tool for justifying whatever actions they take to convert the Soviet Union and the world to communism. The key to this conversion, as Communists emphasize again and again, is education. In building communism, leaders of the Party charge education with two great tasks: first, to produce in accordance with each five-year economic plan sufficient technicians, scientists, and laborers to insure the country's continued growth toward becoming the world's greatest industrial and military power; second, to produce what the Communists refer to as "the new Soviet man," a builder of communism. The new Soviet man has a "Communist world-view." Simply put, a Communist world-view is whatever Party leaders want Soviet citizens to believe at any particular period of time.

There are, of course, some aspects of a Communist world-view that have remained relatively constant over the years since the Bolshevik revolution. Today, as in 1917, the new Soviet man must believe in the basic doctrines of Marxism-Leninism, which may be summarized as follows: 1) There is no spirit; only matter exists. 2) Reality is basically dialectical; that is, everything in the world is interrelated, and necessarily so. 3) The Communist Party and workers have identical aims. 4) Only the Communist Party can lead mankind to communism. 5) Communism will inevitably triumph throughout the world.[4] A person imbued with a Communist world-view will also believe in the glory and dignity of hard work, the greatness of his motherland, the importance of gaining and sharing knowledge, the wickedness of capitalism, the power of science to achieve all of man's aspirations, and the necessity of subordinating his individual needs to the needs of the state. And finally, as M. A. Prokofyev, the current USSR minister of education, puts it, the new Soviet man must believe "that the formation of a world-view is not simply a matter of mastering book wisdom. It is formed through active participation in the life of a collective and in activities that are useful to society."[5]

Such are the new man and woman that Soviet schools must develop. This emphasis of Soviet schools upon development of Communist character, a process generally called "upbringing," is perhaps the most distinctive feature of Soviet education. Producing good Communists is the responsibility not only of the schools, however. As pointed out in the 1973 *Principles of Legislation of the U.S.S.R. and the Union Republics on Public Education*, "Education in the U.S.S.R. is truly a task of the entire people. By joint efforts, the state, the family and the public organizations insure the upbringing and education of the growing generation."[6] Thus, in addition to the schools, the following organizations and institutions are involved in upbringing, i.e., in developing youth with a Communist world-view: Party soviets; professional unions (laborers, technicians, educators, lawyers, doctors, etc.); creative unions (writers, composers, painters, opera singers, etc.); the family; the military; youth organizations; the press; radio; television; libraries; theaters; movies; museums; and art galleries. The kind of influence exerted on Soviet youth by these organizations and institutions is not left to chance. On the contrary, as M. A. Prokofyev points out,

"High moral qualities can be inculcated in an individual only through purposeful actions by the school, family, and community. Success is possible only when all three forces operate in unison and in one direction. . . ."[7] He hastens to add, however, that it is the school, guided by the Party, that must coordinate the efforts of the family and community in the raising of children.

To sum up, the Politburo of the Communist Party controls all aspects of Soviet life, including education. Education is an all-union responsibility, but the schools, as directed by the Party, have the leading role in producing a new kind of person who will not only contribute through his labor to the further development of Soviet industrial and military power, but who will also actively participate in building a Communist society.

The Preschool

Soviet educators and politicians have always paid great attention to preschool education.[8] Lenin considered preschools to be the "green sprouts of communism," providing for the emancipation of women and the social education of children. To Lenin and his present-day successors, social education means education in collectivism. A collectivist—be he 4, 35, or 70 years of age—is one who helps others and who willingly subordinates his interests to those of his collective group. A group that is a collective, in the sense that the Soviets use the term, must have a common goal, but not just any goal. The goal must be to promote the ideals of communism. Since Soviet children are considered active citizens with real responsibilities, a desire to accept responsibility must be inculcated early. For this reason training for active participation in a Soviet collective begins in the preschool. In a very real sense, the preschool forms an essential first link in the formation of the new Soviet man.

Soviet preschools became part of the general education system shortly after the Russian Revolution, and since that time the Soviet Union has developed one of the most extensive preschool programs in the world. Because most mothers hold jobs outside the home, the state, through its network of preschools, has a major responsibility for the education and upbringing of young children.

Although attendance in preschool is voluntary, a number of factors encourage parents to send their children to preschool. It is either free to parents or the cost is minimal. A variety of school schedules comply with the needs of working mothers; there are day groups, night groups, weekend or seasonal groups. There are special schools for children with learning or health problems. The law requires that any enterprise employing more than 500 women must have its own preschool.

Preschools are organized by ages to provide experiences appropriate for each developmental stage of the child. The *yasli*, or nursery school, is for children aged two to three months to three years. Nursery school children are placed in groups (approximately 25 children in each group) according to age level. Children from ages 3 to 7 attend the *detskii sad*, or kindergarten, and are also grouped by age level. The 6-year-olds are placed in a school preparatory group. Sometimes the *yasli* and *detskii sad* are housed in the same building, in which case a child may attend the same school from the age of two months to 7 years.

Education and upbringing (moral development) at the preschool level is a highly planned, orderly process. The state decides what children are to learn and then researchers and pedagogues determine the best and fastest means for accomplishing the learning tasks. Development in the Soviet Union is not expected to "unfold" naturally; the Soviets believe that development can be accelerated by direct instruction. They believe that instruction must begin early and proceed in an orderly fashion. Children are not born with the ability to think; this ability must be developed and shaped to fit the mold demanded by a Communist society.

Children in Soviet preschools receive direct instruction in all phases of development: physical, mental, moral, and aesthetic—from the earliest time possible. The program of instruction and the methodologies for each age child are outlined in detail for teachers.

The *Yasli* School (Nursery School)

For infants, the teachers' guides include: number and times of feedings, time of sleep, baby hygiene, dress and toilet, instructional program during waking hours, and ways to strengthen the baby's body. Adherence to a fixed schedule is deemed essential to assure good health and psychological balance. The instructions are far more detailed than any Western child-rearing book for parents. Speech and concept development are emphasized; crawling and walking are programmed. Listening and responding to music are important aspects of the program. There is a planned sequence for exposure to air, water, and sun for strengthening the baby's body. Collectivism begins by placing infants in group playpens, which are frequently elevated for more eye contact and direct interaction with the teachers and aides.

The development of self-reliance is emphasized during a child's second year. Children become toilet trained and begin to learn to dress, feed, and wash themselves. With their increased ability to walk, much time is spent outdoors in active play and observation of the surroundings. They are taught to observe what adults in the neighborhood are doing and to imitate these activities with their toys. There is an active attempt to relate the children's activities to adult life in society. Children begin to play in groups and learn to share toys. Active speech is stressed and children are taught to generalize and to manipulate objects. Musical and physical activities are increased according to the attention span and ability of the children.

More formal instruction begins at age 2. Strict observance of schedule and regimen continue; each moment is planned so that the children are never placed in the "unhappy" position of having nothing to do and so that time will not be wasted on trial-and-error learning. There is a single schedule for all children in this age group, but the schedule may vary slightly to adapt to individual differences that have resulted from "improper" earlier training. Soviet parents tend to pamper their children, and if children have not attended the infant school, it is likely they have missed some important training. (Soviet educators often talk about the necessity of retraining preschool children.) Instruction in art, music, and physical education begins at this age. Development of all aspects of speech is an important goal. Children are taught to be more aware of their surroundings and to begin to recognize beauty in art, music, and nature. As part of "upbringing" they are taught to clean up their play and work materials, to exchange and share toys, and to engage in many games and activities. The activities are designed for specific educational purposes and require group cooperation. Communal responsibilities begin as children learn to help other children and the teacher. Duties may include helping in the dining room, caring for animals and plants in the classroom, simple gardening, and playground cleanup. In all activities children who do things "right" are praised in front of the group.

By the age of 3, the children have had a variety of planned experiences in social living. Great care has been taken to assure all-round development and the establishment of good health habits. Children have learned to do many things for themselves and to help each other.

The *Detskii Sad* (Kindergarten)

The educational objectives do not differ as children enter kindergarten at age 3, but the activities become progressively more serious and complex each year. During the sixth year children are actively prepared for school through the teaching of basic arithmetic processes and through preliminary instruction in reading and writing.

During the kindergarten years instruction continues in all phases of the child's development, much of it in the form of play. Through role playing, subject play, and construction play, children learn about work and their environment. Games are designed to serve educational objectives and to develop moral qualities and a collective spirit. Play, instruction, and work receive equal emphasis in the kindergarten. Implementation of the pedagogical belief in the value of structuring the entire lives of the children is a distinguishing feature of Soviet preschool. Every activity has an educative purpose, and little choice is left to the child. Choices are not given, because children may choose something they already know or know how to do; the teacher is expected to plan for continuous progress. The children must never become bored by play, instruction, or work; therefore, the teacher must continually introduce more complicated tasks.

A child is ready for school if he can get along with other children and adapt himself to the collective, is physically fit, and has developed basic intellectual skills.

"To know is to love" might be a motto of Soviet education. Children are taught to know music, art, nature, work, and Lenin. Communist morality is learned through work and play in the collective. Love of labor is learned through active involvement in useful work and by becoming acquainted with the work of adults through role playing

13

and on-site visits. Field trips are a daily occurrence in Soviet preschools. Children learn much about their country and Lenin through stories, songs, and pictures.

This brief description of the strict regimen of the Soviet preschool may sound harsh to the Western reader. We should therefore emphasize that underlying all instruction in the Soviet preschool is a tremendous emphasis on the happiness of children. Children are truly valued and loved.

The General Education School

All general education schools in the USSR are public, coeducational, secular, and tuition-free. School throughout the country begins on 1 September and extends to 20 May or into June for those taking eight-year or 10-year leaving examinations. Except in a few republics where the school starting age is 6, Soviet children begin school at the age of 7 and attend a 10-year general education school. The school is usually organized into primary education (grades 1 through 3), incomplete secondary (grades 4 through 8), and complete secondary (grades 9 through 10). It is compulsory for everyone to complete the eighth grade. Upon graduation from the eighth grade, most young people continue in the 10-year general education school. A third of the students, however, go directly to work or enroll in a vocational or technical school. An urban child generally remains in the same school and with the same group of children for either eight or 10 years. A rural child, however, may attend two or three different schools, for a Soviet village often has only one school—a primary school.

What constitutes the educational program between the ages of 7 and 17? Let us look at Soviet education at different levels through the lives of three hypothetical children: Natasha, Ivan, and Svetlana. All three will probably become good Soviet citizens, and Svetlana no doubt will become an active member of the Communist Party.

The Primary School

For the past week or so the news media have featured articles and special programs on teachers and education. Department stores, book stores, and stationery stores are crowded with back-to-school shoppers seeking new uniforms, special lace for dress collars, required notebooks, and pens. September 1 arrives and the flower markets are

15

thronged with parents and children selecting flowers for the teacher. A Soviet school is a kaleidoscope of color and excitement on the first day.

The 7-year-old first-graders are accompanied to school by parents and relatives. Skits and speeches presented by older children welcome the beginners and remind them of the importance of education and of their responsibilities as citizens. The first day of school in the USSR is indeed a big event, symbolizing the reverence most Soviet citizens have for education.

Natasha is 7 and in the first grade. She is assigned to a teacher with whom she will stay until the end of grade 3. Except for special days when she wears her white pinafore, she dresses in a brown dress with a black pinafore. She is well scrubbed and wears her hair either short, braided, or in a ponytail. Natasha attends school six days a week. For two hours a day she studies Russian language, including reading, grammar, spelling, speech, handwriting, and basic composition. Mathematics is studied for one hour per day, and another hour each day is spent on other required subjects. She has art and music instruction once a week and physical education and manual work two hours per week. Classes are 45 minutes each, with a short break between each class. During these breaks Natasha visits with her classmates in the hall or has a snack. She has approximately one hour of homework per night. Grading begins during the second half of her first year; grades range from 1 up to 5. If a child receives too many grades of 2, the school director, parents, and appropriate student organizations are notified. Then the child and her parents are brought to task and a plan of action outlined.

Natasha's classroom is fairly large, with several neat rows of double desks. There are 30 to 40 children in her class and they generally study the same thing at the same time, but some of her friends have more trouble with the work than she does. At the beginning of each lesson the teacher asks questions and Natasha raises her hand, hoping to be called on to stand and recite. She likes to go to the chalkboard and work the arithmetic problems or to be called on to dramatize an important event with her friend Olga. After the recitation is complete, the teacher explains the new lesson and assigns the homework, which Natasha writes down in her notebook. She is proud of her notebook because she usually gets high marks in her subjects and in citizenship, and she likes to have her parents sign the book each week. Her parents do not mind attending the parent meetings because they are never chided for Natasha's work or behavior.

Both of Natasha's parents work, so they enrolled her in the prolonged day school. In the afternoon, Natasha has a hot lunch and plays and does her homework for the next day. She is pleased that her teacher helps with some of her homework because her parents do not really understand all the "new curriculum," although they have attended parent meetings for explanations. In the second and third grades she studies the same subjects, except that she has two hours per week less of Russian and two hours of nature study are added. The amount of homework is increased each year.

By the end of grade 3 the foundation has been laid for all further education. Natasha is well prepared for serious study. She can read, write, and do sums. She has been introduced to nature study and to the geography and history of her country. She has had aesthetic experiences and vocational and physical education training. She can read with expression, take dictation, and use reference books and library catalogues. She can use the multiplication table and has been introduced to set theory and to the sign of inequality.

In grade 1 she became, as did all her classmates, a member of the Octobrist organization, her first Communist youth organization. Being a good Octobrist carries much responsibility. An Octobrist studies hard, likes school and work, is always neat at home and school, shows respect for all grownups, and does the things Lenin would want her to do. Natasha wanted her collective to be the best in the school, so she was truthful as a class monitor even when she had to tell the teacher about the misconduct of one of her classmates. She enjoyed her friends and wanted all of them to follow the rules of the Octobrists. Through literature, music, art, useful work in and outside the school, visits to museums, and field trips in the community, Natasha has learned much about her country and its expectations of her as a citizen.

The Incomplete Secondary School

Ivan enters grade 4 prepared for serious study and work in a difficult curriculum. His classmates are those he has had for three years, but he has new teachers. Except for special subjects, he had the same teacher for grades 1 through 3; now he has different teachers for each subject. He has a class teacher, however, and he knows she will guide his progress for the next four or six years in all subjects and help to organize his out-of-class work. She will take the class to the theater and on a variety of excursions, and she will also keep his parents informed of his progress and behavior.

His curriculum for the next four years includes language and literature, mathematics, geography, and history. He continues to study nature and will start work in biology in the fifth grade, physics in the sixth grade, and chemistry in the seventh grade. He begins a foreign language in grade 5 and mechanical drawing in grade 6. He studies fine arts, singing, and music appreciation. Every year he takes physical education and shop. Beginning in grade 6, he may choose extra subjects, and in grade 8 he takes the new required course in the fundamentals of Soviet state and law.

What is school life like for Ivan? How might it differ from that of Johnny in an American middle school or junior high? They take similar subjects, but there is a stronger emphasis on science and mathematics in Ivan's school. All of Ivan's subjects are required, including shop, foreign language, and mechanical drawing. His electives are extensions of his other subjects and are not recorded on his school leaving certificate. Johnny must stay in school until the age of 16; Ivan is required to complete grade 8, usually at age 15. Ivan may not go on to grade 9 until he has passed the state examinations in his academic subjects. Although Ivan does not receive training for a specific occupation, much attention is given to the value of skilled labor and to acquainting him with different occupations and the relationship between physical and mental work.

The behavior of Ivan and his classmates may be similar to that of students in Johnny's class, but the techniques of discipline will likely differ. Spanking is not only frowned upon in the Soviet Union, it is against the law. Ivan's classmates are supposed to report his misbehavior, and Ivan is then reprimanded by his teacher or his class council. If his misbehavior continues and a reprimand from his principal

18

does not help, school authorities contact his parents. The last resort, and one not frequently used, is a call to the Party organization where his father works. The father is reprimanded for being a bad parent, and that is a disgrace. If he continues to neglect his parental duties, he may lose certain privileges such as a vacation in Yalta, the exclusive Black Sea resort town.

Both Johnny and Ivan arrive at school at about the same time; but if Ivan's class is "on duty," he arrives early and lines up for roll call. He knows his duties, but the teacher on duty and his class teacher will be there to remind him and his classmates to do their work well. And what is their work when they wear the red armband to indicate they are on duty? Members of Ivan's class may meet primary children in the cloak-room to help them with their coats and boots. They may shovel snow or act as hall monitors. They will check to see that the classrooms have been cleaned by the individual classes and assign marks to those re-sponsible for cleaning. They will air the classrooms and see that no one enters the room until the bell rings.

Instead of five days a week, Ivan attends school for six. He changes classes every 45 minutes, with breaks of either 10, 20, or 30 minutes be-tween each class; the longer breaks are for lunch or to visit the canteen. Sometimes the breaks are spent rehearsing for an upcoming play or planning a class party.

Just as in Johnny's school, there are parties, dances, plays, special programs, and concerts. Often a play is followed by dancing, usually the same kind of dancing that Johnny and his friends do. Holidays are celebrated and there is a class party at the end of each school term. In-stead of a Christmas holiday, Ivan has a New Year's vacation. Two holidays unique to Ivan's school and especially enjoyed by older stu-dents are Red Army Day and Women's Day. On 23 February, Red Army Day, the girls congratulate the boys, bring them inexpensive souvenirs such as a squeaky rubber toy, write poems, publish a newspaper, or put on a performance in their honor. On 7 March, Women's Day, the boys congratulate the girls and may also bring toys or honor them in various ways.

The first half of Ivan's school day is spent in class work, the second half is for extracurricular activities. Because of his heavy academic load and up to four hours of homework each night, Ivan is encouraged to participate in no more than two extracurricular activities. His teachers may help him decide which activities will be of greatest interest to him.

Ivan is a member of the children's collective, something unknown to Johnny. It is through the collective, where groups of children work together toward the goals of a socialist state, that Ivan's all-round development takes place. He is a member of his class, school, and various extracurricular collectives. He is a member of the Pioneer organization, a unit of the Communist youth organization for children age 10 through 14. He occasionally joins a temporary collective for a specific project such as a school outing or a school beautification project. In the children's collective, he learns good from evil, his character and attitudes toward work are formed, political development takes place, and his behavior in public and private are controlled. Johnny may be called a "tattletale" for reporting misbehavior of his peers; Ivan is encouraged to do so. Ivan soon learns that he must subordinate his own interests and needs to those of the collective.

Ivan's school is called a polytechnical labor school, as are all Soviet secondary schools. This means that not only is Ivan to acquire basic scientific knowledge, but he is to learn how this knowledge is applied in an industrial society and also to apply it in projects appropriate for his stage of development. For example, he learns carpentry and metal work and works on various projects in electricity. He learns agricultural skills and applies these skills on the school garden plot. Through such activities, it is hoped that Ivan will learn to value the relationship between mental and physical labor. It is the responsibility of each of his subject teachers to apply the principles of polytechnical education to instruction.

Another unique aspect of Ivan's school, and closely related to the polytechnical training, is labor education. Work training began for Ivan in the preschool, where he made toys or other useful items, was on duty in the lunchroom, or was responsible for the care of plants or animals. He continued work appropriate for his age in the primary school. Now that he is in secondary school, work training is of a more serious character. Through the coordinated efforts of the school and the young Communist organizations, Ivan receives training and experience in a variety of socially useful tasks both inside and outside the school. Not only does he participate in the care of the school and school grounds, but he may join teachers and other adults to plant trees, clean parks, and beautify neighborhoods. He may join a student work brigade for a specific project such as helping with the harvest. In all of Ivan's subjects and activities, the emphasis will be on preparing him to make his contributions to a socialist society. He must study hard and work hard.

In grade 4, Ivan, unlike Johnny, has approximately two hours of homework each day; he has up to four hours in grade 8. In spite of the required homework, Ivan, like Johnny, engages in a wide variety of after-school activities. He skis, cycles, ice skates, plays soccer and other ball games, and occasionally goes horseback riding. Two or three times a week he goes to the Pioneer Palace, where he engages in activities related to his abilities and interests. He may join the chess club, a sports or art club, or any number of technology and science clubs. There are clubs for every interest, and they are led by experienced teachers, scientists, chess masters, or other experts. Beyond the Pioneer Palace, Ivan may join interest clubs organized by different children's extracurricular establishments, such as the Young Naturalists or Young Technicians.

In order to go on to grade 9, Ivan must pass the eighth grade examinations. Academically, Ivan is a fairly good student, making 3s, 4s, and 5s in all his subjects, so he will be permitted to take the examinations. Since he did not make all 5s and his conduct was not always exemplary, he will not receive an honor certificate, but if he passes all his oral and written examinations, he will graduate and receive an eight-year certificate that gives him the right to enter the ninth grade. At this point, however, he must make a choice as to the kind of school he will attend. He may enter the ninth grade of a general education school, where he would attend grades 9 and 10 to complete his secondary education. He may enter a vocational school to become a skilled worker or go to a combination secondary-vocational school, where he would prepare for a vocation and get a secondary education. Or he may apply for entrance to a technical or specialized secondary school and, if he passes the entrance exams, be trained as an "intermediary" specialist or technician, such as a primary school teacher, a doctor's assistant, a building technologist, or a technologist for some other branch of industry. Ivan, like most of his classmates, will probably enter the ninth grade of a general secondary school because it is the best route to a higher education. The best way to get ahead in Ivan's society, as in Johnny's, is through higher education rather than vocational or intermediate technical training.

The Complete Secondary School

Svetlana is an example of what the new Soviet person should be. Two years ago she graduated from the incomplete secondary school with grades of 5 in all subjects. She took to heart Lenin's admonition to "study, study, study," and she was a leader in her class and in the school collectives. For her academic diligence and good citizenship she was awarded an honor certificate at the end of the eighth grade. She is now completing the tenth grade of the complete secondary school. She has studied exceptionally hard and continues to be active in "socially useful" work, for she is well aware that only one in 10 of the secondary school graduates will be accepted into the day division of an institution of higher learning, and she wants more than anything else to be a research chemist.

In the ninth grade Svetlana continued to study subjects introduced in the fifth and sixth grades. For an elective she enrolled in a special chemistry class reserved for outstanding young scientists. She was introduced to a variety of vocations, and she had experiences in practicing a number of useful skills, both practical and technical. She learned to cook and sew, which she enjoyed, but she envied male classmates who participated in military exercises and who spent one day a week learning to operate machinery at a nearby factory.

In the tenth grade Svetlana was introduced to two new subjects: astronomy and social science. In astronomy she most enjoyed visiting the Moscow Planetarium, which was within walking distance of her school. In social science she learned of the evils of capitalist production and the values of the socialist mode of production. She also gained an appreciation of the essential role of the Communist Party in making the Soviet Union a great nation and in promoting the international Communist movement. She completed a systematic study of history

22

from ancient times to the present. As a result of her historical studies, she now has a "scientific" understanding of the laws of social development as set forth in the teachings of Marx and Lenin. Since most of her teachers taught their subjects from a polytechnical perspective, she learned how her knowledge of science and mathematics could be applied to industrial production and the betterment of life in general. Having studied English for five years, she has acquired considerable knowledge of the United States, especially about how capitalists exploit the working man.

Svetlana has now been a member of the Komsomol (the Young Communist League) for almost two years. She will serve in this organization until she is 28, at which time she will apply for membership in the Communist Party. Her experiences as a Pioneer, especially at summer camp, convinced her that she wanted to help carry out the work of Lenin. When she became a member of the Komsomol, she was well aware that she had accepted a strict obligation to help the Party build communism and that much would be expected of her in the future. She realized that it was her duty, more than ever before, to set an example for younger children so that they might be attracted to the building of a Communist society. She has worked hard the past two years to set a good example. She engaged in socially useful work during her day off from school and during holidays. She worked with Pioneers and often assisted adults in extended day schools by taking the young children for walks or reading to them and playing with them. She was not afraid to report misbehavior or bad study habits at collective meetings. In all of her acts she was guided by the principle, "not I and mine, but we and ours." Through the Komsomol and the polytechnical labor education, she has learned to love labor and to respect as equals the working man and woman who create the material wealth of her country. Unlike some of her friends who joined the Komsomol only because it was the "thing to do" or because it would help them get ahead later in life, Svetlana really believes in the high ideals of the Komsomol organization, and she wants to do her part, as a Soviet citizen, to put these ideas into practice.

It is now nearing the end of June and Svetlana has just completed her school-leaving examinations. As everybody expected, she received all 5s on her examinations. At the graduation party she will be awarded a gold medal "for excellent achievement in studies and work and for exemplary conduct." The gold medal will allow her special privilege in applying for higher education. Her school-leaving certificate gives her the right to enter a technical school or a secondary specialist school (for a shorter time than those who entered after grade 8) or to apply for an institute or university. Her choice is the university, and unlike most of her classmates she has a good chance of being admitted, for her gold medal attests to her diligence as a student and to her potential for making a valuable contribution to society as a professional.

Svetlana looks forward to the graduation party; not all of her classmates do. Those who failed subjects were not permitted to take the state examinations. Classmates who received an unsatisfactory mark in conduct were barred from the examinations. In order to take the tests, they must present, within the next three years, a good character reference from their place of work. Classmates who failed one or two of the state subject examinations will not receive their matriculation certificate with the class, but they will be allowed to retake the tests before the next school year or again the following year.

In conclusion, all Soviet students are, of course, not as ideal as Svetlana, Ivan, and Natasha, nor are all schools identical to those they attended. The curriculum is standard throughout the Soviet Union, but, just as in America, there is considerable difference among schools, students, and teachers. The Soviet Union is not without its educational problems.

Problems

In publications designed for foreign consumption, Soviet educators, politicians, and journalists seldom criticize their educational system. When they write for Soviet citizens, however, they are candid about their educational problems. In newspapers, journals, and books they often discuss such problems as excessive homework; lack of instructional aides and equipment in many schools; the wide gap that exists between the quality of education in urban and rural areas; the "scornful attitude" of many older students toward social science studies (those that extol the virtues of communism); the reluctance or inability of many teachers to utilize "progressive," "creative" methods of teaching; and the lack of interest on the part of both parents and students in vocational and intermediate technical training. Coping with this last problem is especially important to Soviet leaders at the present time, for the USSR is suffering a severe personnel shortage. To alleviate this shortage, the Party in a recent resolution has instructed educators to improve labor education and vocational guidance and to provide students with a vocational skill that can be utilized immediately upon their entrance into the labor market.[9]

In closing we should point out that Soviet educational critics, unlike some American critics of education, constantly stress that reform of schools must start with reform of the education of teachers. As a *Pravda* editorial writer has noted, "The chief factor in the school is the teacher, his ideology and breadth of his vision, his skill and creative inspiration. Betterment of the training and refresher programs for teachers was one of the tasks laid down at the Party Congress for the tenth five-year [1975-1980] period."[10] Since editors, politicians, and educators in the USSR place so much emphasis on teacher education, the next chapter discusses the training program for Soviet teachers.

Teacher Education in the USSR

The products of teacher education institutions in the U.S. and the Soviet Union are quite different. American teachers represent every shade of political and religious thought. Perhaps for this reason they are not expected to assume direct responsibility for the moral development of the students in their classes. Such responsibility has traditionally belonged to the family and church. In contrast, a Soviet teacher must either belong to the Communist Party or be committed in word and deed to its work. In addition, he must be a militant propagandist of atheism and be the primary agent—even more so than the family—for developing the moral character of his students. In short, the ideal Soviet teacher (preschool, elementary, or secondary) must provide for children and youth a model of the new Soviet man or woman. Secondary school teachers have an additional responsibility. While a secondary school teacher is expected to know his subject well and to teach it effectively, his first and most important responsibility is to serve as a propagandist of party ideology. To prevent any misunderstanding about the priority of this function, F. G. Panachin, the deputy minister of the USSR Ministry of Education, declared a few years ago that "the core of the entire educational and indoctrinational process in the pedagogical institutions of higher education is the training of the young teacher to fulfill an indoctrinational mission in the school and in society. Pedagogical institutions of higher education must train [each student as] *a teacher-indoctrinator, a teacher-propagandist, and a teacher-activist engaged in public life.*"[11]

The major goal of teacher education in the Soviet Union, then, is to mold all teachers into models of the new Soviet man or woman, and in addition, to produce secondary school teachers who are active propagandizers of party ideology. To produce such teachers, the Party has developed a wide network of teacher preparation institutions that includes pedagogical schools, pedagogical institutes, and universities.

Structure

To be admitted to a Soviet institution that prepares teachers, a person must have a good academic record and favorable character references from teachers and classmates. In addition, he must pass an examination given by the institution to which he is seeking admission. Deciding to which institution to apply is a very serious business for a prospective teacher, because admission standards of different institutions vary considerably and an applicant may apply to only one institution during any one year. If an institution turns down an applicant, which happens frequently, he must wait a year before applying again to another.

The great majority of Soviet elementary teachers are trained in pedagogical schools. These are specialized secondary schools that offer a four-year course for graduates of the eight-year general education school, and a two-year course for graduates of the 10-year general education school. Half of the four-year course is devoted to courses provided in the ninth and tenth grades of the general education school. The two-year course is devoted exclusively to professional education work. While pedagogical schools are the main vehicle for training elementary teachers (as well as kindergarten teachers, youth organization leaders, and grades 4 through 8 teachers of art, music, and physical education), an increasing number of the elementary teachers are now being trained in pedagogical institutes that have departments of elementary education.

Secondary teachers are educated in pedagogical institutes, universities, and other institutions that specialize in the training of artists, musicians, and specialists in foreign languages and physical education. Only graduates of the 10-year secondary school or its equivalent may seek admission to these higher education institutions. The course of study is four years for those seeking certification in one academic subject, five years for those seeking certification in two academic subjects. Over 60% of all teachers are certified in two subjects.

Pedagogical institutes are single-purpose institutions; that is, they train only teachers. Universities are multipurpose institutions that train not only school teachers and professors but also specialists who conduct research in many areas of basic and applied science. Although most secondary teachers are trained in pedagogical institutes, nearly 20% are trained in universities. In universities, as compared with pedagogical institutes, more emphasis is given to providing the prospective teacher with research skills and a more thorough preparation in one or two academic subjects. In addition, universities offer the teacher candidate much less in educational psychology, theory, and methodology. The amount of student teaching experience is also less than in pedagogical institutes.

Upon completion of their professional preparation in a school, institute, or university, teacher candidates must then prepare for a state examination. Elementary teachers are tested on the theory, history, and practice of pedagogy and on their knowledge of and ability to teach their native language, mathematics, and social studies. Secondary teachers are tested on knowledge of their subject and their ability to teach it, on the fundamentals of "scientific communism" and on their knowledge of the theory, history, and practice of pedagogy.

If the teacher candidate passes the state examination, he is assigned to a school for a one-year probation period. Only after successfully completing the probation period does he become a certified teacher. Thereafter, he must be recertified by the state certification commission at five-year intervals. This commission assesses not only the teacher's teaching and upbringing work but also his "moral make-up," involvement in the social life of the school and community, and the extent to which he has improved his professional qualifications. At any time during the recertification process, teachers judged best by the commission may be awarded the title of "senior teacher" or "teacher-method specialist."

Program

Professional courses in pedagogical schools include the following: anatomy, physiology and hygiene of school children, educational psychology, child growth and development, history and philosophy of education, children's literature, and methods of teaching the various elementary-level subjects. Considerable time is also devoted to drawing, modeling with clay, workshop training (working with wood, metal, etc.), physical education, and lessons on a musical instrument, such as a piano, violin, or accordion.

In pedagogical institutes, the curriculum consists of three major divisions: social sciences, psychological-pedagogical sciences, and specialized sciences. Social science courses are: history of the Communist Party, political economy, dialectical and historical materialism, scientific atheism, and the foundations of scientific communism. These are required courses, and students in a four-year program devote 454 hours to them; those in a five-year program, 544 hours. Subjects classified as psychological-pedagogical sciences are: introduction to education, history of education, general psychology, school hygiene, growth physiology, growth and pedagogical psychology, methods of upbringing work, scientific organization of the teacher's work, teaching technology, and methods of teaching various subjects. Most of these courses are required, and students devote 460 hours to them. Specialized sciences are those subjects that comprise a student's area of academic specialization. Approximately 2,000 hours are devoted to study of specialized sciences.[12]

Students in pedagogical institutes are also required to take a foreign language and to participate in various seminars devoted to such topics as current problems of didactics and the theory and methods of upbringing. As a prerequisite for graduation, they must submit a "diploma project" on a topic related to either principles of education or methods of teaching.

The training of Soviet teachers is not restricted to academic work. Students in pedagogical schools and institutes are required during the first two years of their training to serve as teachers' aides in a nearby school. During the summer of their second and third year, they serve as supervisors in youth camps, generally Pioneer camps. In their last two years they spend 16 to 20 weeks becoming familiar with the operation of schools, supervising extracurricular activities, tutoring pupils, and teaching lessons.

Prospective teachers are also expected to engage in "socially useful" labor. They participate in the political activities of the Komsomol organization, organize concerts, give lectures to parents on pedagogical topics, and participate in various kinds of conservation campaigns and community beautification projects. Many also join various student work brigades during the summer. A work brigade may do such things as help construction workers in the Far North build a hydroelectric plant or help collective farmers in the Ukraine harvest their crops. Experience in these brigades is an important factor in the "upbringing" of future teachers. As one Soviet educator put it, "This summer work, which has come to be known as the Labor Semester, is of great importance to the students' ideological and political development, in preparing them for teaching in the schools, in realizing the principle of maintaining close ties between studies and life, with the actual building of communism."[13]

Inservice Education

As in the U.S., much attention in the Soviet Union is now being given to inservice education of teachers. While there are many reasons for this attention in the USSR, three stand out as especially important.

First, there are at least 1,250,000 Soviet teachers and upbringers who do not have higher pedagogical training, that is, training at the institute or university level.

Second, as a result of the nationwide curriculum reform movement and the transition to compulsory 10-year general education, teachers are expected to individualize instruction and to improve their teaching methodology. Contrary to what one might think, Soviet educators are now talking as much as American educators about the necessity of meeting the "individual needs and interests of students" and the importance of a teacher gaining a "deep understanding" of how children develop mentally. Soviet educators also talk about the importance of developing a student's "independence and initiative." These educators are quick to point out, however, that "the chief means toward gaining this end is the children's collective, which is capable of satisfying the many needs and interests of its members, of helping in the all-round development of each individual and bringing out and encouraging each child's talents and abilities."[14]

Third, as a result of the transition to universal 10-year education, Soviet pedagogues point out that on one hand most of their young people are becoming increasingly knowledgeable, sophisticated, and inquisitive. On the other hand, some older students, who 10 years ago would have been employed full time in a collective farm or factory, are often indifferent if not actively hostile to everything associated with school. Discipline, it seems, is becoming a serious problem in many Soviet schools, especially in schools located in blue-collar districts. For both groups of students, the easy answer no longer suffices, so say Soviet pedagogues. In professional journals and textbooks pedagogues constantly stress that if a teacher is to instill in his students a desire to learn on their own and if he is to motivate them to live according to Communist principles, he must himself become each year a more knowledgeable person, a person who knows not only his subject but related subjects and all aspects of the science of pedagogy.

To retrain teachers to cope with these and other demands of the modern world, the Soviet Union has developed a comprehensive program of inservice education. As mentioned earlier, all Soviet teachers are required to be recertified every five years. In doing the work necessary for recertification, a teacher may draw upon one or more of a large number of different kinds of institutions. He may take work in one of the 200 evening or correspondence divisions of pedagogical institutes or may enroll in courses offered each year by pedagogical schools and institutes, universities, and other higher education institutions. In addition he may take work in one of the country's 228 people's universities of pedagogical knowledge, 250 homes for workers of enlightenment, or 178 institutes for the advanced training of teachers. We should point out that not all these institutions are equally accessible to all teachers. Rural teachers, for example, generally must rely heavily on correspondence work.

Soviet elementary and secondary schools are in session six days a week, but teachers are expected to devote one of these days to self-improvement activities provided by the organizations and institutions just mentioned. For some self-improvement activities, teachers are given leaves of absence with pay.

Problems

At the undergraduate level Soviet teacher education shares a number of problems in common with American teacher education. Like American teacher educators, Soviet pedagogues are concerned that many of their students have no interest in teaching but only want a degree. They regret, along with their American counterparts, that institutional politics are such that their students (particularly university students) are provided inadequate opportunities to teach school children, the result being that many beginning teachers enter the classroom with little idea of how to adjust subject matter to the individual needs and interests of students at a particular stage of development. Soviet pedagogues also join American teacher educators in lamenting the fact that the low salary and poor working conditions of teachers discourage many highly competent people, especially men, from either entering or remaining in the teaching profession. This latter problem is especially acute in the Soviet Union. While it is true that Party leaders constantly praise teachers as being the key to producing a Communist paradise on earth, the fact remains that teaching in the USSR is a very low-paid profession, much more so than in the U.S. Teachers with five years of higher education often make less money than a common laborer with only eight years of general education. A middle-level technician with the equivalent of our junior college education may make two or three times more money than the typical teacher in the USSR.

Working conditions for Soviet teachers are also more difficult than those imposed on American teachers. As pointed out above, the Communist Party insists that teachers do much more than teach academic material to their students. Some idea of the incredible demands imposed on Soviet teachers may be gleaned from the following complaint by a Soviet teacher to the editor of a professional journal:

> "GO ON DUTY, PLEASE!" Yes, yes, that's what I. A. Tropin, the city Soviet executive committee chairman, said to us teachers. Twice a month we are supposed to arrive at the militia station punctually at 7 p.m. to go on duty as volunteer militia aides—our tour lasts until 11.
>
> I must say that the teachers don't refuse when they are called upon to help in one situation or another. But here we are talking about a permanent additional duty.
>
> We started counting up the number of immediate tasks we have each month. During the second quarter, for example, on 43 working days we

had: a teachers' meeting, a production meeting, a conference of home-room teachers, a methods association session, lectures for teachers, two lecture series for parents, four political study classes, two schoolwide Young Communist League meetings and two Young Pioneer detachment assemblies, four meetings of hobby groups concerned with school subjects—and I have listed only the most important extracurricular activities.

Our school operates on two shifts. For this reason, a great deal of work has to be left until after the final bell. What, for instance, is put off until evening? Meetings of the parents' committee, and the pupils' committee, conferences with the principal, visits to pupils' homes, lectures, political information sessions at enterprises, field trips with the children to movie theaters, etc.

It is the duty of each teacher to conduct daily upbringing work—that is, to be in charge of meetings, debates, evening gatherings and student matinees, readers' conferences, olympiads, and homeroom time.

I haven't even mentioned that lesson preparation at the level of to-day's demands and the checking of pupils' notebooks take considerable time. Besides, a teacher should constantly engage in self-education. This again hinges on time. Add to this the fact that teachers are mostly women, who have responsibility for the care of their families and households.

There are three schools in our city. The "schedule" is this: For six days a month the teachers "patrol" the evening streets, and on the other 24 days the miners and construction workers do it.[15]

Commenting on this letter, the editor said, "Letters of this sort, un-fortunately, are frequent in our mail. The teacher's time is a critical problem. . . ."

We should mention another factor that may deter many of the more gifted young people from entering the teaching profession in the USSR: the demand that teachers inculcate in youth a Communist world-view. This factor, of course, is never alluded to in public by pedagogues or teachers. While an engineer or scientist may go about his business without thinking much about ideology or worrying about being a model of the new Soviet man, there is no escape for the teacher. He is always on center stage with a bright spotlight. He must be a model of the new Soviet person, and he must insist that his students emulate, in word and deed, the good example he sets. It is a reasonable assumption that many talented young Soviet men and women who would like to be teachers avoid the field because they are well aware that teachers must also teach their students "truths" that do not coincide with the real world. The world these young men and women know, for example, has rigid classes and little freedom of speech, religion, or movement. Yet, they were taught by their teachers that the USSR is a classless society and that Soviet citizens have more freedom of speech, religion, and movement than any people in the world. For many of these young people teaching such "truths" would be a demeaning experience that would compromise their intellectual integrity.

Soviet pedagogues, of course, must give attention to some problems that generally receive little or no attention by most American teacher educators. They work very hard, for example, to resolve the problems associated with preparing teachers for infant schools, boarding and prolonged-day schools, and secondary vocational-technical schools. Their most complex problems, however, are: 1) how to train a large number of teachers to work in rural schools that serve approximately 50% of the nation's population; 2) how to instill in these teachers a commitment to devote their lives to teaching in rural areas. At present the government must literally force most teacher graduates to work in rural communities. By law all teachers must teach their first three years in a school designated by the government, after which time, presumably, they may seek employment elsewhere. While we have no hard data, comments by pedagogues in journals, books, and newspapers strongly suggest that first-year teachers are invariably dispatched by the government to remote villages where living conditions are exceptionally difficult and opportunities for cultural fulfillment very limited. Their comments also suggest that it is a rare teacher who chooses to remain in a village school after completion of his required three-year term of service.

Making rural life attractive for Soviet citizens and teachers is a very serious national problem to which Party leaders have given much attention over the years. Until it is resolved, Soviet pedagogues will continue to struggle with how to train 50% of their graduates to work in rural schools and how to motivate them to continue working in such schools once they have a choice as to future employment.

Educational Accomplishments

While there is presently a certain disenchantment with U.S. public school education, most Americans in the past 100 years have been passionately devoted to their public schools. In their view the public schools have "Americanized" millions of immigrants, abolished illiteracy, provided the trained manpower to make America the leading industrial power of the world, and promoted the democratic way of life reflected in their Constitution. With equal justification the Soviets are proud of the many accomplishments of their educational system.

It is difficult for Americans to comprehend how culturally backward Russia was prior to the 1917 revolution. We think of the great nineteenth-century Russian novelists and composers and wonder how it was possible for a backward country to have produced such creative geniuses as Turgenev, Dostoyevsky, Tolstoy, Glinka, Rimsky-Korsakov, and Tchaikovsky. Nevertheless, in comparison with most Western European countries of the day, Russia was a cultural wasteland. On the eve of the revolution most Russians were illiterate and impoverished. The dual-track system of education meant, with a few exceptions, that only the privileged class got a higher education. The privileged class, we should point out, was quite small. Most of the nobility were just as impoverished and ignorant as the peasants, who comprised the great bulk of the population and who still lived much as they had prior to their emancipation from serfdom in 1861.

Today, illiteracy in the Soviet Union is negligible. Practically everybody has eight years of general education, and the great majority of the younger generation has had 10 years of general education. Some form of advanced education is now available to most 10-year school graduates who have the ability to profit from it. Opportunities for life-long learning are provided by a wide variety of different institutions, in particular the so-called people's universities, which are large public lecture centers where anyone may attend a free lecture course on such areas of study as aesthetics, literature, art, history, political economy, natural sciences, and international relations.[16]

In addition to increased educational opportunities, concerts, plays, ballets, and operas are inexpensive and accessible to the common man in the larger cities. Such cultural opportunities in the villages, of course, are limited. Nevertheless, the Soviet village is not nearly as isolated culturally as the old Russian village. Practically every home in a Soviet village now has a radio or a television set, and the government makes a real effort to send to rural areas touring symphony orchestras and ballet, theatrical, and operatic companies from large cultural centers such as Moscow and Leningrad. Also, the number of libraries and museums has increased dramatically since the revolution, and books are inexpensive and accessible to Soviet citizens. It is a rare community that does not have a bookstore of some kind.

While the USSR today is not a cultural paradise, it is no longer a cultural wasteland. The nation's schools and other educational institutions have indeed raised significantly the cultural level of the Soviet people. Furthermore, the education system has provided the trained manpower that has enabled the USSR to become one of the world's great industrial and military powers. These are not small accomplishments, but the ultimate goal of Soviet education—to form a new Soviet man and woman—remains elusive. Constant demands by Party and educational leaders to improve the upbringing process strongly suggest that many Soviet citizens are not imbued with a Communist world-view. Only time will tell if the Soviet Union can actually transform human nature and develop a nation of people committed heart and soul to whatever world-view is espoused by Party leaders at a particular time. We note here only that it will be a formidable task. For one thing, the Russian character gets in the way. Classic Russian writers such as Fyodor Dostoyevsky would probably agree with the following recent assessments of Russian character:

No state tries harder to make its people "active fighters in the ranks of our Party's universal-historical struggle"; and no people has a greater

36

natural resistance to [this] kind of mobilization and regimentation. In a vague way, most of them believe what they are taught. They are strong Russian patriots and happy with strong leadership. But they are politically passive, undeveloped, uninterested.[17]

If sentimentality is the counterpoint to Russian stoicism, then the folksy, traditional, peasant ways of Russians are the antithesis to the inflated rhetoric of Marxism-Leninism about the new Soviet man. Not only are Russians easygoing, indolent, and disorganized rather than scientific, rational, and efficient, but they are as simple and homespun in their leisure as their friendship. Martyrs of self-denial they may be in time of crisis, but otherwise they are lusty hedonists, devoted to such sensual pleasures as feasting, drinking, and bathing. And in open contradiction to the strictures of scientific socialism, they are a mystical, religious, superstitious people at heart.[18]

No matter how formidable the task, we should not discount the determination of Soviet leaders to produce a new kind of person. As was recently pointed out in a book by two Soviet sociologists, "Marxists-Leninists firmly oppose the idea that human feelings and morals cannot be reformed. Moreover, the history of socialist society refutes this idea. Radical social reforms in the Soviet Union have created the objective conditions for profoundly changing Soviet people's moral make-up."[19]

Notes

1. Quoted in Hedrick Smith, *The Russians* (New York: Quadrangle/New York Times Book Co., 1976), pp. 234-235.
2. Quoted in George S. Counts, *The Challenge of Soviet Education* (Westport, Connecticut: Greenwood Press, 1975), p. 47.
3. Quoted in Michael T. Florinsky, *Russia: A Short History* (London: The MacMillan Company, 1969), pp. 666-667.
4. Our discussion of the fundamentals of Marxism-Leninism draws heavily on Richard T. DeGeorge, *Patterns of Soviet Thought: The Origins and Development of Dialectical and Historical Materialism* (Ann Arbor: University of Michigan Press, 1966), pp. 226-248.
5. *The Current Digest of the Soviet Press* 30 (8 February 1978): 7.
6. *The Current Digest of the Soviet Press* 25 (29 August 1973): 31.
7. M. A. Prokofyev, "Problems of the School under the Tenth Five-Year Plan

in Light of the Decision of the Twenty-Fifth Congress of the CPSU," *Soviet Education* 19 (November 1976): 85.

8. In preparation of this chapter we have drawn upon the following sources: N. Kuzin and M. Kondakov, eds., *Education in the U.S.S.R.* (Moscow: Progress Publishers, 1977); N. Aksarine and N. Smirnova, *Social Education of Preschool Children in the Soviet Union* (Moscow: Novosti Press Agency Publishing House, 1975); Henry Chauncey, ed., *Soviet Preschool Education, Vol. 1: Program of Instruction; Vol. 2: Teacher's Commentary* (New York: Holt, Rinehart and Winston, Inc., 1969); several Soviet pedagogical books that have not been translated into English; *Soviet Education*, a monthly journal of translations published by M. E. Sharpe, Inc.; *The Current Digest of the Soviet Press*, a weekly journal published by the American Association for the Advancement of Slavic Studies; our personal impression of Soviet schools in action during the 1975-76 academic year and also during the spring of 1977; interviews with Soviet citizens, including teachers and students.

9. "On Further Improving the Teaching and Social Education of General Education School Pupils and Their Preparation for Labor," *Soviet Education* 21 (April 1979): 8-20.

10. *The Current Digest of the Soviet Press* 28 (5 May 1976): 31-32.

11. F. G. Panachin, "Urgent Problems in Teacher Training in the Ninth Five-Year Plan," in *Soviet Education* 15 (July 1973): 14. Panachin's book, *Teacher Education in the U.S.S.R.: Historical Development and Current Trends*, is an invaluable source of information about Soviet teacher education. This book has been translated into English and was printed in its entirety in *Soviet Education* 19 (July-August 1977). In writing the chapter on teacher education, we have drawn upon Panachin's book, articles in *The Current Digest of the Soviet Press* and *Soviet Education*, and sections on teacher education in a number of Soviet pedagogical books that have not been translated into English.

12. F. G. Panachin, *Teacher Education in the U.S.S.R.: Historical Development and Current Trends*, p. 201.

13. P. V. Zimin, "The Soviet Teacher," in N. Kuzin and M. Kondakov, eds., *Education in the U.S.S.R.*, p. 143.

14. G. V. Berezina and A. I. Foteyeva, "Educational Work and Extra-Curricular Educational Establishments," in N. Kuzin and M. Kondakov, eds., *Education in the U.S.S.R.*, p. 73.

15. *The Current Digest of the Soviet Press* 30 (8 February 1978): 7, 24.

16. R. Reshetov and V. Skurlatov, *Soviet Youth: A Socio-Political Outline* (Moscow: Progress Publishers, 1977), pp. 134-135.

17. An Observer, *Message from Moscow* (New York: Vintage Books, 1971), p. 241.

18. Hedrick Smith, *The Russians*, pp. 112-113.

19. R. Reshetov and V. Skurlatov, *Soviet Youth: A Socio-Political Outline*, p. 150.